T0034195

Table of CONTENTS

What Is Dirt? 4
Types of Dirt 8
Layers of Dirt 14
Who Lives in Dirt? 18
What Do We Use Dirt For? 22
How Can We Take Care of Dirt? 24

Dig In! 28
Glossary 30
Read More 31
Internet Sites 31
Critical Thinking Questions 32
Index 32

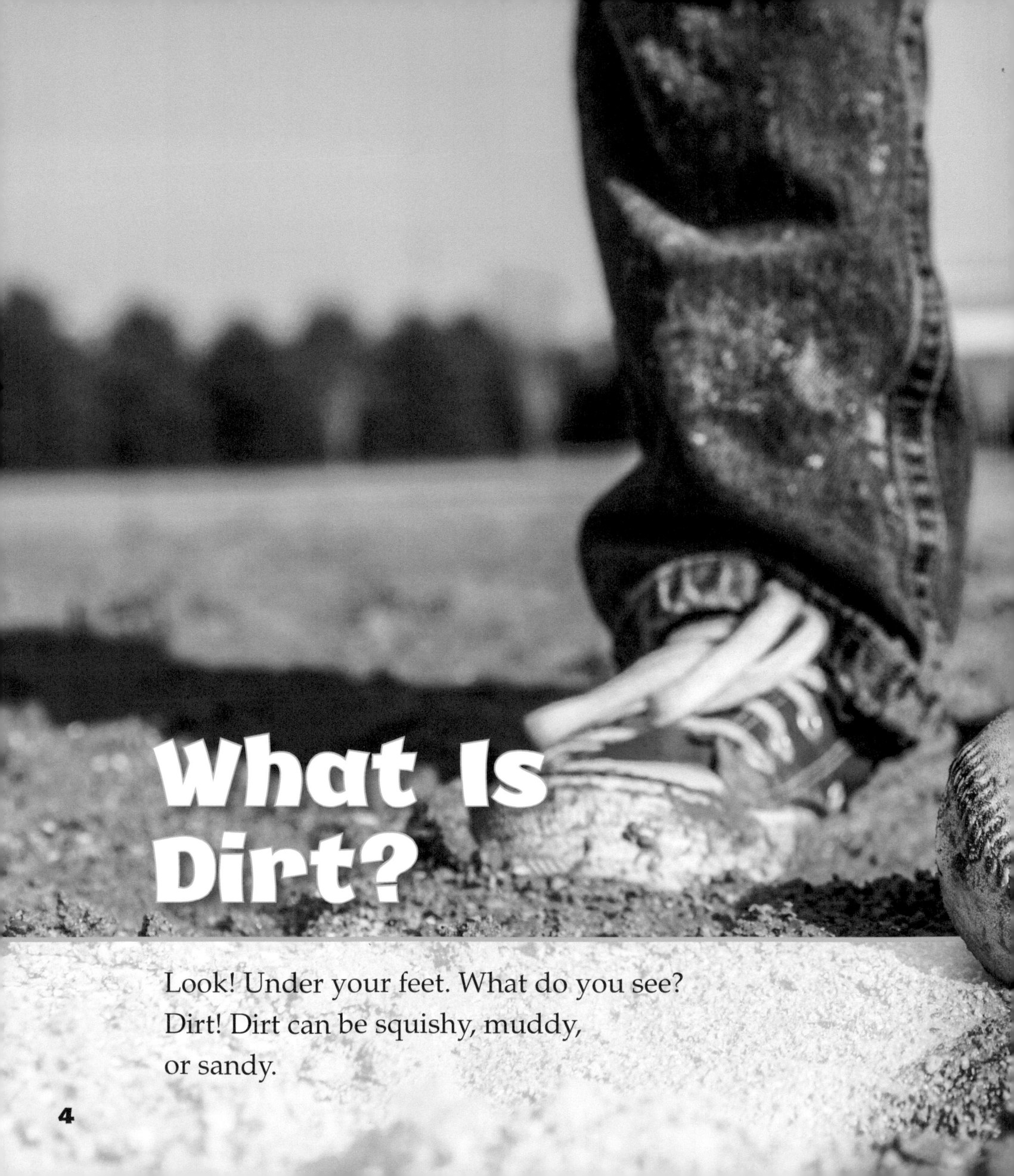

What Is Dirt?

Look! Under your feet. What do you see?
Dirt! Dirt can be squishy, muddy,
or sandy.

SIMPLY **SCIENCE**

The Simple Science of DIRT

by Emily James

CAPSTONE PRESS
a capstone imprint

A+ Books are published by Capstone Press,
1710 Roe Crest Drive, North Mankato, Minnesota 56003
www.mycapstone.com

Copyright © 2018 by Capstone Press, a Capstone imprint. All rights reserved. No part of this publication may be reproduced in whole or in part, or stored in a retrieval system, or transmitted in any form or by any means, electronic, mechanical, photocopying, recording, or otherwise, without written permission of the publisher.

Library of Congress Cataloging-in-Publication Data
Cataloging-in-publication information is on file with the Library of Congress.
ISBN 978-1-5157-7085-5 (library binding)
ISBN 978-1-5157-7092-3 (paperback)
ISBN 978-1-5157-7100-5 (eBook PDF)

Editorial Credits
Jaclyn Jaycox, editor; Jenny Bergstrom, designer; Jo Miller, media researcher; Tori Abraham, production specialist

Photo Credits
Shutterstock: Alexander Bark, 8-9, Antonov Roman, 16-17, dnaveh, 26-27, Dragon Images, 24-25, Drakuliren, 22-23, Elvan, 21, Fabio Lamanna, 10-11, fotoslaz, 28-29, GalapagosPhoto, cover, George Dolgikh, 14-15, LexRiver, 7, marcovarro, 18-19, MR.RAWIN TANPIN, 6, Nick Biemans, 20, Riccardo Arata, 12-13, showcake, 13 (inset), spiphotoone, 23 (inset), Sujalmages, 29 (inset), Suzanne Tucker, 4-5

Design Elements
Shutterstock: diogoppr, xpixel

Note to Parents, Teachers, and Librarians

This Simply Science book uses full color photographs and a nonfiction format to introduce the concept of dirt. *The Simple Science of Dirt* is designed to be read aloud to a pre-reader or to be read independently by an early reader. Photographs help listeners and early readers understand the text and concepts discussed. The book encourages further learning by including the following sections: Table of Contents, Glossary, Read More, Internet Sites, and Index. Early readers may need assistance using these features.

Printed in the United States 5947

You can dig, play, and plant flowers in it.
Dirt covers almost all the land on Earth.
But what is dirt?

Dirt is also called soil. Soil is a mix of different parts of nature. Rocks form one part. Sand, silt, and clay are pieces of rock that make up soil.

Pieces of leaves and twigs also make up soil. So do tiny parts of animals that lived long ago.

Types of Dirt

Soil found near the ocean is usually made of sand. Sand is mostly broken-down rocks and shells. It feels rough and gritty.

Sand has large grains. They do not stick together well. Water drains quickly through sandy soil. This soil does not have many nutrients. They are carried away by water.

Silt is like sand. But silt's grains are smaller. It is a dark color. It feels soft and smooth. Silt is a good soil for growing plants. It holds a lot of food and water for plants.

Clay has even smaller grains than silt. It can be many colors. It feels soft and sticky. Clay does not drain well. Minerals stick to it. Minerals make clay a good soil for growing crops.

Humus is the dark, gooey part of soil.
It is made from rotting plants,
leaves, wood, and animal matter.

Sticky humus helps hold the rocky parts of dirt together. Humus contains food that plants need to grow.

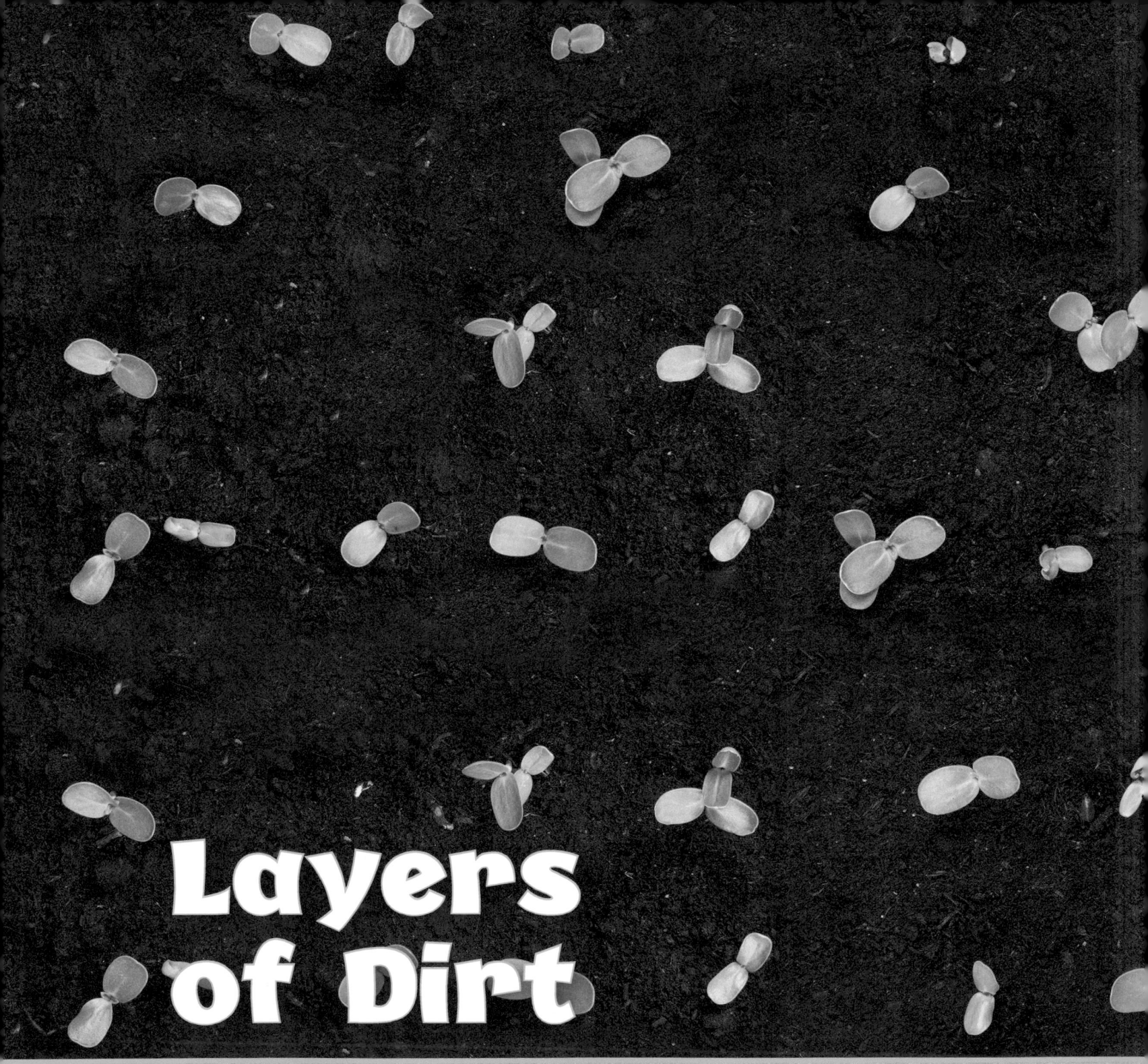

Layers of Dirt

Humus, water, and air are usually found in the upper layer of dirt. This layer is called topsoil.

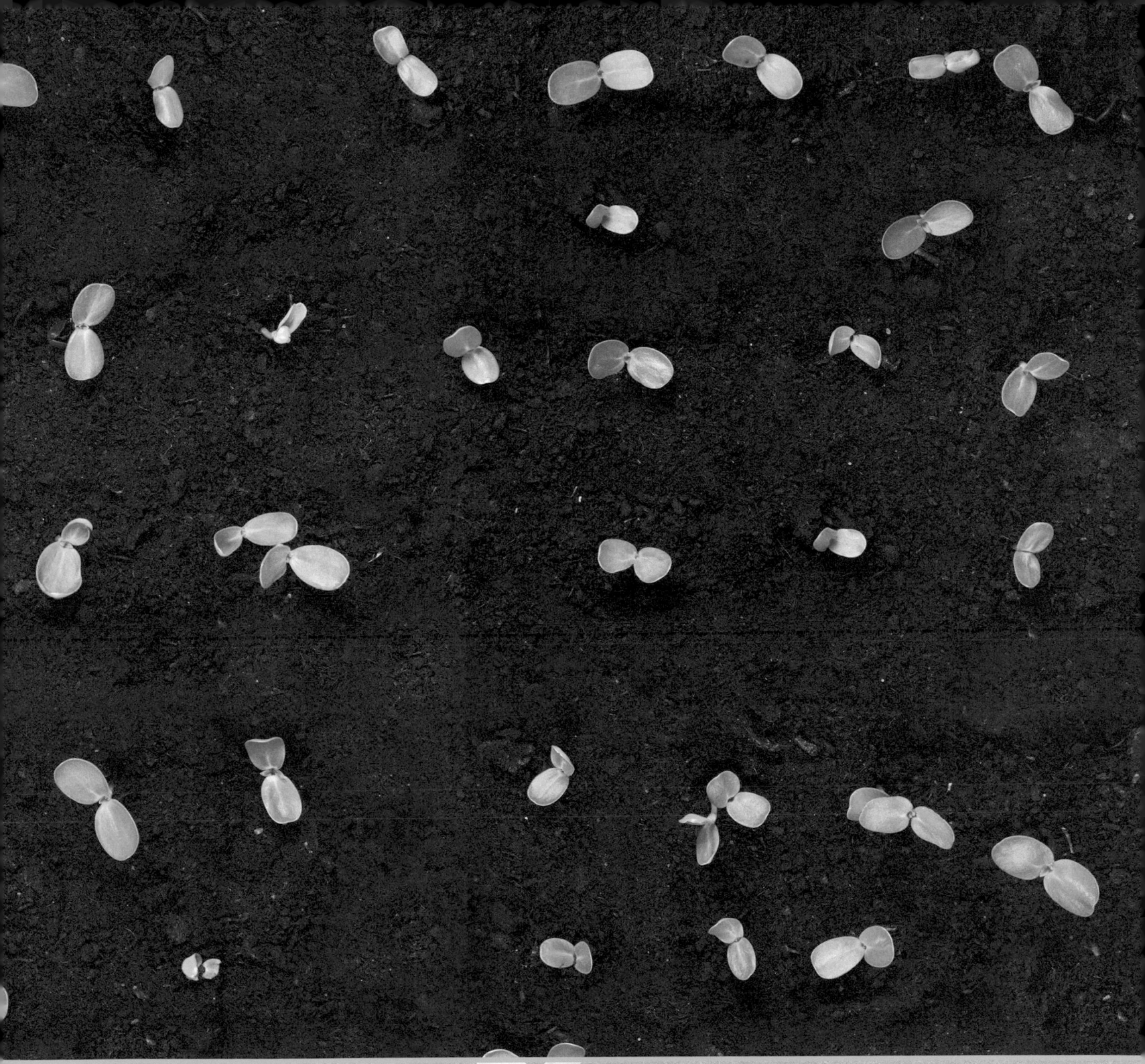

Topsoil is very dark and filled with nutrients. It is the best soil for planting. Topsoil can take hundreds of years to form.

Under topsoil is subsoil. Minerals gather in this layer. The roots of plants reach into subsoil for food and water.

Deep below subsoil is solid rock.
No plants or animals live in this layer.
Soil forms from this rock.

Who Lives in Dirt?

Millions of creatures live in dirt. Beetles, millipedes, and worms wriggle and crawl through it. Many decomposers are so small that you can't see them.

Decomposers make humus. They eat dead plants and leave droppings in the soil. The droppings are like vitamins for plants.

Animals can make soil better for plants. Snails, snakes, and rabbits burrow into soil and loosen it.

They make holes that let air and water reach the roots of thirsty plants.

What Do We Use Dirt For?

People use dirt for many things.
Farmers use it to grow crops.
Engineers use it to build roads and dams.

Clay soil is used to build houses.
Sand is used to make cement.

How Can We Take Care of Dirt?

Plant trees! Roots hold soil together. Without trees, soil can be washed or blown away. Leaves help protect soil from too much rain.

Don't litter! Trash can harm soil, plants, and animals. Keeping soil healthy is good for all living things.

Dirt keeps us alive. Without dirt, plants cannot grow. Without plants, animals cannot eat. Without plants and animals, people would have no food.

Dig into dirt. Pile it up and stomp it down. Plant flowers in it. Let it squish between your fingers and toes. See how amazing the world beneath you is!

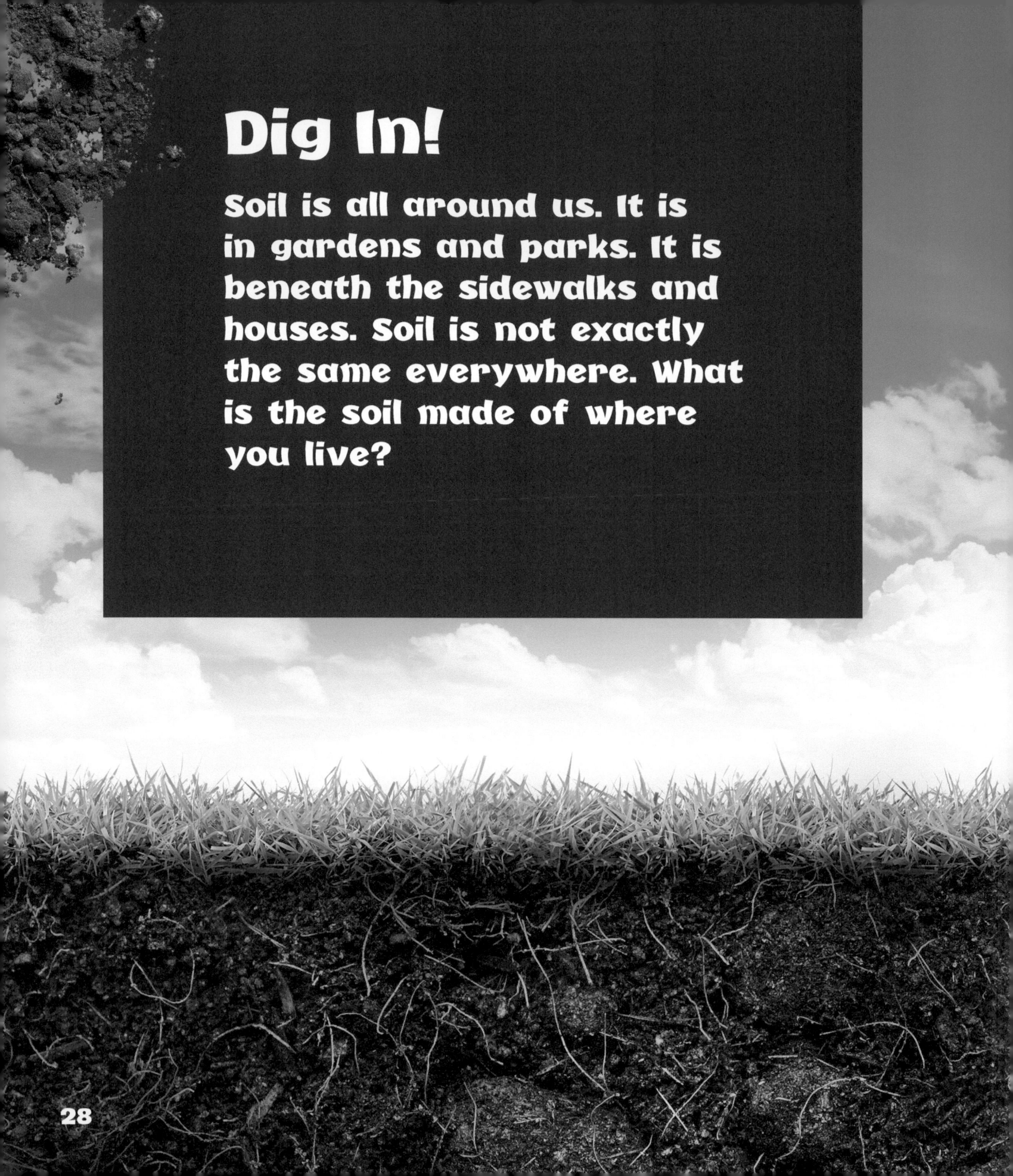

Dig In!

Soil is all around us. It is in gardens and parks. It is beneath the sidewalks and houses. Soil is not exactly the same everywhere. What is the soil made of where you live?

What You Need:

shovel

white paper plate

What You Do:

- Have an adult help you dig up one shovelful of soil. Make sure you dig down deep to get more than just the topsoil.
- Put the soil on the paper plate and spread it out.
- Look for leaves, sticks, bugs, worms, and rocks. Make a list of all the things you find.
- Pour some water on the area where you dug up the soil. Does the ground hold a puddle for a long time? Or does the water sink right away? What does that tell you about your soil?

GLOSSARY

cement—a gray powder made from crushed limestone and clay

creature—a living being

decomposer—a living thing, such as fungi or bacteria, that feeds on dead plants and animals and turns them into soil

engineer—a person who uses science and math to plan, design, or build

grain—a very small piece of something

humus—the wet, dark part of soil that is made of rotted plants and animals; humus has food that plants need

mineral—a material found in nature that is not an animal or a plant

nutrient—something that is needed by people, animals, and plants to stay healthy and strong

silt—the fine particles of soil that are carried along by flowing water and eventually settle to the bottom of a river or lake